Original title:
The Paradise Pathway

Copyright © 2025 Creative Arts Management OÜ
All rights reserved.

Author: Franklin Stone
ISBN HARDBACK: 978-1-80581-669-0
ISBN PAPERBACK: 978-1-80581-196-1
ISBN EBOOK: 978-1-80581-669-0

Chasing the Celestial

In the sky, a donut flies,
With sprinkles bright, oh what a prize!
We chase it up, we chase it down,
Can't catch it — what a silly frown!

A cow in shades shimmies near,
Sips sweet tea, has no fear.
It tips its hat, gives us a grin,
Then takes a leap, we can't win!

Meadows of Merriment

In fields where daisies dance and sway,
The rabbits run a cabaret!
They wear tiny shoes, tap their feet,
While squirrels cheer, now isn't that neat?

A sunbeam slides down, cracks a joke,
While flowers giggle, a laughing cloak.
A bee in glasses, oh what a sight,
Buzzing puns in sheer delight!

Wooded Wonders

In woods where trees wear silly hats,
The owls sing songs with funny spats.
A fox recites, a bear beats drums,
Together make strange forest hums.

A picnic's spread, with pies that float,
Squirrels mime, on a comedic note.
And every step, a laugh will bloom,
In this wild, whimsical room!

Gates of Grace

At gates of joy, a jester waits,
With juggling pies, oh what greatmates!
He winks and twirls, such quirky flair,
While giggling flowers sway in air.

Behind the gates, a dance unfolds,
With silly moves, everyone holds.
Painted zebras, what a parade,
In laughter's hue, our cares just fade!

Enchanted Elements

In a forest where squirrels dance,
They wear tiny hats, take a chance.
The mushrooms giggle, the trees all sway,
A parade of laughter, hip-hip-hooray!

The rivers gurgle jokes so bright,
Splashing water, a comical sight.
A frog in a tux hops by with style,
His bowtie flutters, quite the profile!

Veil of Verdant Vistas

Green hills roll like laughter's tune,
Under a sky, the color of June.
A bear on a bike, oh what a scene,
Pedaling past, wearing sneakers so green!

Butterflies dance with glittering flair,
In this realm, all have the time to spare.
A rabbit juggles carrots, so very sly,
While a turtle takes selfies, oh me, oh my!

Dreamscapes Unveiled

Upon a cloud with candy floss,
Ideas bounce like a playful toss.
The moon wears shades, as stars all wink,
Cosmic jokes that make you think!

A dragon in joggers, fleet as a breeze,
Chasing rainbows with the greatest of ease.
In this land where dreams collide,
Laughter's the key, no need to hide!

Path of Promised Peace

On this road, where laughter blooms,
Chickens wear clashy, colorful plumes.
While bunnies skip and twirl away,
Chasing giggles, oh what a play!

Sunshine bursts in hues so bright,
Tickling toes, bringing pure delight.
With a friendly ghost who cracks a pun,
This whimsical path is just pure fun!

Marvelous Mosaic

In a garden where flowers wear hats,
Bumblebees dance like acrobatic cats.
Sunflowers gossip, tall and grand,
As daisies giggle, hand in hand.

A squirrel slides down a candy cane,
Pigeons play poker in a sunflower lane.
The carrots have disco balls at night,
And radishes wear sunglasses, what a sight!

Trails of Tranquility

On the road less traveled, right past the creek,
Frogs wear top hats, oh so chic!
The trees are talking, they mumble and sway,
While turtles tell tales of their slow, sweet day.

A raccoon plays cards with a wise old owl,
Beneath a sky where the stars love to growl.
Breezes laugh softly, tickling the leaves,
While the moon winks at those who believe.

Rustic Reveries

In a barn where the goats hold a dance,
Chickens wear mittens, oh, what a chance!
The hay in the loft whispers stories of old,
While cows sing ballads, their voices so bold.

A pig on a tricycle, racing so fast,
With a chicken as DJ, spinning tunes from the past.
Barn doors are flung wide, laughter abounds,
As the rabbits bring snacks and jump all around!

Gentle Waves of Whimsy

On a beach where the crabs wear big shoes,
Seagulls serenade the ocean blues.
Shells hold meetings, discussing the tide,
While starfish play poker, so dignified.

A fish with a bow tie does a dance,
Snapping his fins in a fancy romance.
The waves giggle softly, tickling the shore,
As the sun bows deeply, asking for more.

The Secret Symphony of Hidden Paths

In the forest, trees hold trumpets,
As squirrels play the xylophone, oh yes!
With mushrooms waltzing to a tune,
And frogs crooning to a soft breeze.

Rabbits tap dance on a stage of grass,
While hedgehogs hum as they pass.
A cacophony of joyful beats,
Nature's band will never cease.

Bumblebees buzzing a sweet refrain,
While ants march on like a train.
The whole wood sings with glee,
Creating notes we cannot see.

So grab your hat and join the show,
Where laughter sprouts and joy will grow.
In this secret, wild concert we glean,
Life's a laugh on this leafy green!

Flora Dancing to an Endless Rhythm

In the meadow, flowers sway, oh my!
Daisies waltzing, raising petals high.
Tulips twirl in a splendid dress,
Carnations giggle, oh what a mess!

Buttercups bounce with glee, it seems,
As dandelions blow their fluffy dreams.
Each bloom's a dancer on nature's floor,
They're spinning round, begging for more!

Bees are the DJ, buzzing loud,
While ladybugs sway, oh they feel proud.
With every breeze, the petals bend,
A floral fiesta that never ends!

So if you wander where flowers play,
Join their dance, don't shy away.
Nature's ball is quite the affair,
With blooms galore, joy fills the air!

Beneath the Canopy of Infinite Skies

Underneath this leafy dome so wide,
Birds chirp jokes while kittens hide.
Monkeys swing on branches high,
Sharing secrets with the butterfly.

The clouds chat in fluffy delight,
While sunbeams giggle, oh what a sight!
A picnic party with ants in tow,
Nibbling crumbs and putting on a show.

Squirrels gossip about acorn finds,
While raccoons dance, leaving trails behind.
With a wink from the moon up high,
They all sing ballads as stars nearby.

So if you desire a laugh or two,
Beneath the trees, there's fun for you.
In this playground of nature's brew,
Joy awaits, just step on through!

Glimpses of Tranquility on a Wandering Heart

A path of pebbles leads to glee,
Where wishes float on each small breeze.
Butterflies parade in vibrant hue,
While munching on sweet ambrosia too.

A wandering soul hums a sweet tune,
With clouds above playing peek-a-boo.
The laughter of streams is a joyful sight,
As stones skip along in sheer delight.

With each step, joyous echoes grow,
In the sunlight's warm, golden glow.
Glimmers of joy dance by the trees,
Life's grand comedy, carried on the breeze.

So if you find a quiet place,
Let laughter bloom, or pick up the pace.
With every smile, peace takes part,
In this journey of a wandering heart!

The Lure of Timeless Horizons

To chase the sun with glee, we run,
Chasing shadows, having fun.
Yet clouds giggle, whispering low,
'Oh dear, where'd your time go?'

With time machines made of bubble gum,
We hop and skip, a silly drum.
But clocks just laugh, they play their tricks,
And we're left puzzled, doing silly kicks.

Celestial Footprints on Earth's Canvas.

We danced beneath a goofy moon,
Twinkling stars sang a silly tune.
With each step, we left behind
Footprints where laughter intertwined.

The grass tickled our wiggly toes,
While hopscotch turned into a pose.
A comet crashed — don't worry, mate!
It's just the sprinkle of a cosmic fate!

Elysian Escapade

We packed our dreams, a jolly spree,
On unicorns we rode with glee.
The fruit trees danced in dizzy spins,
Kicking back as laughter begins.

Jellybeans rained from skies so blue,
Sipping sunshine — oh, what a view!
Chasing rainbows on a merry path,
Stopping only for a friendly laugh.

Garden of Whispers

In a garden where giggles bloom,
Whispers float like candy perfume.
Plants dressed in hats, oh what a sight,
Telling jokes 'til the day turns night.

The flowers wink with cheeky flair,
As butterflies dance without a care.
Each leaf chuckles, swinging with zest,
In this funny world, we find our best.

A Voyage Through Enchanted Realms

We set sail on a shoe-sized boat,
With candy canes and a rubber goat.
The fish wore hats, the turtles danced,
In a jellybean sea, we all entranced.

A walrus juggled with clams galore,
While penguins played on the sandy shore.
We dreamed of ice cream and cotton candy,
As gnomes served tea, oh so dandy!

Traces of Serenity in the Wilderness

In the woods where squirrels read books,
And the trees wear sneakers, oh what looks!
The owls hoot jokes that make us giggle,
While rabbits rave and do the jiggle.

Nature's all dressed in sparkly charms,
With comfy clouds and formless farms.
The squirrels debate on the best nut stew,
And one lost a bet, now wears a shoe!

Gentle Echoes of an Ancient Trail

Walking down paths with a bounce in my step,
With frogs wearing cloaks; what a curious rep!
The bugs play cards under mushrooms, it seems,
In this trail of laughter and whimsical dreams.

A fox in a bow tie gives us a nod,
And a snail's on a skateboard; how utterly odd!
We chase butterflies that play tag in the air,
In this silly vista, oh how we care!

Unraveling Wonders in Nature's Embrace

Oh, the flowers are singing, what a surprise!
While the daisies don glasses, looking so wise.
Bees in tuxedos pull chariots bright,
As crickets compose tunes throughout the night.

The moon is a disco ball, spinning with glee,
While raccoons decide they'll join in for tea.
The owls all sport monocles, sipping their brew,
In this wild party where all's askew!

Ethereal Embrace

In a realm where daisies laugh,
Bunnies wear their finest scarf.
Dancing clouds in silly twirls,
Butterflies with wigs and pearls.

Silly squirrels in tiny hats,
Juggling acorns with the bats.
The sun winks in a cheeky way,
While flowers cheer and sing hooray!

Lush Landscapes

In fields where cucumbers wear shoes,
And mushrooms boast the latest news.
A frog teaches a toad to sing,
While hedgehogs play a game of bling.

The grass just tickled my bare feet,
As ants parade in brave defeat.
A picnic with a twist of glee,
With sandwiches that dance and flee.

Glories of the Grove

In trees where apples wear a crown,
And lazy hippos dance around.
Chatty crows with gossip spree,
Tell tales of bees and jubilee.

Bright oranges in yoga class,
Bouncing peaches with a laugh.
While acorns on a roller skate,
Declare the day is truly great!

Voyage of Vibrance

A river sings a merry song,
As turtles join the dance along.
Ducks decked out in carnival gear,
Prance and quack with silly cheer.

Giggling rocks rolled down the slope,
As jellybeans give dreams of hope.
A rainbow train whirls on through,
Inviting all to join the crew!

Tryst with Tranquility

In a land where daisies dance,
Laughter twirls in bright romance.
Squirrels giggle, winds do swirl,
While sunbeams play, like kids they whirl.

Butterflies plot a secret scheme,
To paint the air with colors' dream.
They joke with bees, who buzz and tease,
In this realm where all hearts seize.

Mushrooms wear their tallest hats,
Whimsical as gossiping cats.
Frogs in tuxedos leap and slide,
In a pond where joy can't hide.

So come rejoice, just take a seat,
Join the fun, it's quite the treat.
Leave your troubles, let them be,
In this realm, we're all carefree.

Echoes of Elation

Bouncing bunnies hop with glee,
Chasing shadows, silly spree.
Acorns roll like little toys,
Echoing the laughter of boys.

Clouds above wear faces bright,
Tickling raindrops, pure delight.
Each splash brings a merry cheer,
As puddles beckon, come near.

Daisies whisper witty tales,
Of playful winds and whimsical gales.
Frolicking folk, they dance and spin,
In a world where smiles begin.

With every step, let joy take wing,
Sing with crickets, let hearts swing.
A echo of pure delight does play,
In this enchanted, happy way.

Ethereal Expedition

On a journey through the sky,
Pink elephants wave and fly.
With umbrellas and balloons,
They sing out silly, happy tunes.

Carefree clouds with cotton candy,
Doodle dreams that taste so dandy.
Wobbling rainbows, flip and flop,
While giggles make the raindrops stop.

Bubbles float, they bounce and tease,
Chasing shadows among the trees.
Squirrels wear their party shoes,
And dance beneath the shining ooze.

So let's embark on this grand quest,
An adventure that feels the best.
With every laugh and every cheer,
Join in the fun, it's crystal clear.

Boughs of Benevolence

Under boughs of giggling trees,
Whispers float upon the breeze.
Chirpy birds play hide and seek,
With silly songs, they play the cheek.

Breezy wind in polka dots,
Skips over fields in merry knots.
Grass tickles toes that run about,
With laughter bursting, joy's the shout.

Friendly clouds in hat and coat,
Drift on laughter's merry boat.
Casting shadows, warm and bright,
Giggling stars in fleecy light.

So dance on leaves, don't miss the fun,
Underneath the jolly sun.
In this realm where kindness grows,
Silly antics steal the show.

Celestial Wayfarer

A traveler floated on a cloud,
With sandals made from stars so loud.
He tripped on a comet, oh what a fuss,
Landed in a nebula, riding a bus.

The sun winked at him, what a tease,
While moonbeams chortled among the trees.
He wore a hat of cheese so bright,
Gathering giggles, a comical sight.

Planets danced in a cosmic jig,
While he played hopscotch with a big pig.
They laughed at the dark, stole sunlight's shine,
In the galaxy's playground, all was divine.

But on that path, with humor as fuel,
He learned that laughter makes stars cool.
So off he went, on a giggled spree,
In the universe's embrace, wild and free.

Labyrinth of Light

In a maze spun of glitter and beams,
A jester pranced in colorful dreams.
Chasing shadows that danced with glee,
He tripped on a ray and fell on his knee.

The lanterns giggled and gave a wink,
As he pondered why shadows could drink.
With a grin, he asked, 'Where's the juice?'
They replied, 'In laughter, there's always a use!'

He rode a beam like a bike made of gold,
With jokes about sunsets, daring and bold.
A mirthful chase through a radiant door,
The light made him chuckle, always wanting more.

Through twists and turns where it's easy to grin,
He found joy in chaos, let the fun begin.
With every step in the magical maze,
He danced through the light, in a humor-filled blaze.

Flora and Fauna Trail

On a trail where flowers wore shoes,
And rabbits played poker with wild kangaroos.
A squirrel spun tales of nutty delight,
While the sun set, painting laughing sights.

The flowers whispered jokes to the bees,
One said, 'Why do birds fly with such ease?'
They chuckled and buzzed, a sweet serenade,
On this whimsical path, fun was displayed.

The trees joined in with a riddle or two,
The ferns giggled softly, their laughter like dew.
While mushrooms capered with sprightly cheer,
Every step echoed giggles, loud and clear.

As critters convened in their forest parade,
With daisies and daisies, a jovial charade.
They knew on this trail, with a chuckle and jest,
Life's greatest gift was simply the best.

Enchantment Underfoot

Beneath the ground, where the gnomes take naps,
Lies a path of laughter, sprinkled with taps.
They tickle the roots and wiggle the dirt,
Creating a chorus of giggles and mirth.

With mushrooms like umbrellas, they skipped in line,
Casting giggly spells by the old twisted pine.
Fairies flitted, sprinkling joy as they flew,
And the whole forest chuckled, 'Oh, how we grew!'

The daisies danced and the toadstools leaped,
While a curious hedgehog snored and then peeped.
'Wake up!' cried the pixies, 'Come join the fun!'
And the hedgehog smiled, 'I've missed everyone!'

As they twirled and spun on this magical way,
The ground held secrets of laughter each day.
For beneath our feet, in the soil so deep,
The laughter of nature stirs dreams from sleep.

Whispers of Eden's Trail

In a garden filled with candy,
I tripped over a jellybean.
Looked around, feeling dandy,
A squirrel in a tutu, quite the scene.

Flowers giggled as I strolled,
Singing tunes of silly glee.
With each step, the laughter rolled,
Even the bees danced joyfully.

A frog played chess with a cricket,
Each move a ponderous delight.
I joined in, tried not to pick it,
Checkmate—who knew frogs could fight?

As the sun took a bow to the night,
I found a path made of candy forks.
With a grin, I took my flight,
On chocolate clouds with gummy storks!

Steps Through Celestial Gardens

Among flowers with faces so bright,
I danced with a cat wearing shades.
It purred in the shimmering light,
Claimed it was the king of charades.

Butterflies played tag in midair,
While daisies cheered from below.
A tulip asked if I would dare,
To join them in their flower show.

As I twirled, I lost my shoe,
A gopher borrowed it for style.
He said, 'These look good, who knew?'
I laughed, shared my jokes for a while.

Night wrapped the gardens in glow,
With stars chuckling overhead.
I waved to a snail moving slow,
He winked back, his face all red!

Journey to the Luminous Horizon

On a quest for the prisms so bright,
I rode on a turtle, quite spry.
He boasted he raced with the light,
But moved at a snail's pace, oh my!

Clouds showered confetti of fun,
While rainbows danced without a care.
I thought I'd outshine everyone,
'Til I slipped on a banana—oh dear!

With socks that sparkled in sun,
I hopped, leaving giggles in air.
A parrot squawked, "You're the one!"
His feathers, a riot, beyond compare.

When I reached my bright destination,
I found jelly sandwiches in stacks.
The horizon held a celebration,
Where dreams and snacks never lack!

Dreams Woven in Sunlight

In fields where shadows tickle the ground,
I met a rooster who could sing.
He claimed his voice was famous, renowned,
But sang off-key—oh, what a fling!

Squirrels traded nuts for some cheese,
While rabbits threw marshmallows high.
Laughter floated on the breeze,
As butterflies giggled and flew by.

A picnic was laid under trees,
With sandwiches made from green goo.
I took a bite, fell to my knees,
"Delicious!" I shouted, "Just for you!"

As bright stars twinkled at dusk,
We danced 'round a fire of glow.
With friends and fun, we built trust,
In twilight's embrace, joy would flow!

Serenity's Journey

A duck in a hat with a cane,
Strutted down the lane with no strain.
He quacked a tune, oh so bright,
Even the moon chuckled in delight.

A hedgehog wearing shades so cool,
Joined the duck, breaking every rule.
They danced beneath the goofy trees,
Doing the twist in a gentle breeze.

A cat on a skateboard rolled by,
Gave a wink and a playful sigh.
"This journey's weird, but never dull!"
Said the duck with a chuckle and pull.

Their laughter echoed through the glade,
Where silly shadows were gladly made.
With every step, their joy would grow,
In this whimsical world, how the fun would flow!

Through the Veil of Blossoms

A squirrel in a dress spun 'round,
While bees drummed up a joyful sound.
Petals fell like confetti in spring,
As butterflies danced in a colorful fling.

A frog with a trumpet hopped near,
Playing jazzy notes, oh so clear.
The flowers giggled, their colors shone,
Together forming a band of their own.

A bumblebee queen took a sip,
Of nectar from a flower's lip.
She jived and waved her tiny crown,
In this garden, she'd never frown.

Through branches woven like sweet dreams,
Every creature burst at the seams.
With chuckles echoing everywhere,
Life was fun without a care!

Gateway to Bliss

A penguin in shades slid down a hill,
With ice cream cones, they had a thrill.
He shouted, 'Whee!' with a giggle and cheer,
As snowflakes danced, drawing near.

A bear tried to dive but missed the slide,
Land into a snowbank with a goofy glide.
The fans, all gathered, roared with glee,
'Who's the king of fun? Well, it's definitely thee!'

A twirling otter sported a bow tie,
He challenged a seal to give it a try.
Together they flopped with glorious grace,
Rolling in snow, a messy embrace.

With each bright chuckle, they dared to play,
In the land where silliness ruled the day.
Every moment bursting with bliss,
In a frosty wonderland, you couldn't resist!

Luminous Horizons

In the land of glow, where fireflies meet,
A snail wore a glowstick, oh what a feat!
He slid with style on the path of light,
Exclaimed, "I'm the spark of the night!"

A rabble of rabbits hopped with delight,
Colorful glasses reflecting the night.
Their little dance shone like stars,
While giggling and jiving beneath Jupiter's bars.

A gopher played hopscotch on fluffy clouds,
As joyous laughter erupted in crowds.
Each step released a flickering glow,
In this whimsical world, joy would flow.

The horizon twinkled with every breath,
Silly moments defying sweet death.
Lighthearted antics lit up the skies,
A dazzling feast for childish eyes!

Arc of Aesthetic

In a world where ducks wear hats,
And cats breakdance on purple mats,
The sun plays peek-a-boo in the sky,
As squirrels fly by on a pie-shaped pie.

Rainbows burst in goofy dance,
While flowers giggle at their chance,
To tickle bees with silly jokes,
As butterflies join in, oh what hoaxes!

Clouds wear shoes that squeak and slide,
While rabbits hop in synchronized stride,
And every step sprouts laughter loud,
An aesthetic dream that feels so proud.

So join the fun, don't miss the play,
Embrace the quirks of this wild ballet,
For life's a joke wrapped in a spin,
A funny tale where smiles begin.

Secret Sanctuaries

Behind the trees where shadows twirl,
There lives a gnome who loves to whirl,
He juggles mushrooms, oh what a sight,
While squirrels cheer with pure delight.

The whispers of the leaves have sass,
As bunnies perform a tightrope class,
Amidst the giggles of secret streams,
They turn our frowns to silly dreams.

In cozy corners where mischief brews,
Frogs tell stories with wild reviews,
Each echoing laughter a sweet delight,
In playful realms from morn till night.

So take a stroll on grassy lanes,
Where wacky wonders always reign,
With every step, let laughter burst,
Embrace the charm that leaves you cursed!

Haven of Hues

In a garden filled with rainbow paint,
Where flowers dance like a gossiping saint,
The sun wears shades, cool as can be,
As butterflies sip tea on a dandelion spree.

Chickens don tuxedos, what a show!
While ladybugs poker-faced, steal the glow,
It's a colorful chaos, a vibrant flair,
With crickets singing karaoke on the air.

Here, even raindrops wear silly hats,
Each splash of color, a giggling cat,
The world's a palette, dripping glee,
In a haven where laughter runs free.

So step inside this quirky land,
Where shades of humor go hand in hand,
Giggles bloom in every hue,
In a canvas where the fun is true.

Glistening Goals

With wobbly smiles, we aim for stars,
As jellybeans jump in candy cars,
The moon winks with a cheeky grin,
While marshmallows laugh, ready to spin.

In this light, dreams bounce like balls,
As giggly echoes dance through walls,
Cactus hats and comet tails,
Create the path where humor prevails.

Each step we take, the giggles bloom,
As penguins in tuxes clear the room,
For every stumble, there's a cheer,
Chasing glistening goals, oh dear!

Now come along, don't be shy,
Join the fun, let's soar and fly,
In this space where dreams take strolls,
Life's just a jest, with glistening goals!

Songs of Radiance Along the Way

In a world where giggles bloom,
Flowers dance, dispelling gloom.
Bees wear shades, a stylish crew,
Buzzing tunes of joy anew.

Squirrels breakdance on the floor,
Claiming acorns, wanting more.
Dancing ducks have great appeal,
In this place where laughs are real.

Rainbows glimmer, skies turn bright,
Making even clouds feel light.
With a chuckle and a cheer,
Every step brings fun near here.

In this realm of painted smiles,
Happiness flows for miles and miles.
Join the chorus, sing along,
Life's a scrolling comic, not too wrong!

Illuminated Dreams in Soft Footfalls

Whimsical whispers ride the breeze,
Where even shadows giggle with ease.
Fluffy clouds in a tickled daze,
Float like pillows in sunlit haze.

Caterpillars wear tiny hats,
While butterflies play silly spats.
Sipping nectar, sipping tea,
In a garden of jubilee!

The rabbit wears a vibrant tie,
Conducting bunnies as they fly.
Oh, what fun in this bright jam,
Field trips with a side of ham!

Every step is new delight,
As the stars twinkle in the night.
Laughter echoes in soft tones,
Marking paths where joy has grown!

Awakening to Ethereal Landscapes

In a realm of cotton candy skies,
Where giggles bloom and humor flies.
Cats in capes and dogs that sing,
Life's a riot, just look at spring!

Mice with jokes are taking bets,
On who will lose, or get the nets.
While pancakes dance on sunny grills,
And syrup rivers climb the hills.

Butterflies strut in polka dots,
While frogs show off their crazy spots.
Jellybeans roll with a cheeky grin,
As friendship blooms with a silly spin.

Every sunrise is a wild show,
Where laughter lives and breezes blow.
Step on in, the fun's on tap,
In this land of oohs and awh-apps!

Luminous Reflections of a Gentle Mind

In a meadow where whimsy reigns,
And laughter flows like gentle rains.
A wise old owl on his perch,
Crafts silly tales and jokes that search.

Frogs play chess, the stakes are high,
While flies buzz round like they can fly.
Sunflowers nodding, head to beat,
With dancing roots beneath their feet.

Clouds tickle the moon's bright face,
While stars waltz in a slow embrace.
A gentle breeze tells secret dreams,
In a world where nothing's as it seems.

The merry-go-round of joy spins fast,
Filling days with love that lasts.
Put on your hat, join the fun,
In the realm where laughter won!

A Walk Amongst Seraphic Blooms

In fields where daisies wear a hat,
The bees throw parties, how about that!
Butterflies dance with a silly grace,
I tripped on a root, what a funny place!

Sunflowers giggle, their heads so tall,
Their laughter echoes, a whimsical call.
I asked a rose for a fashion tip,
It threw a thorn, that's quite a quip!

Dandelions puff like tiny clouds,
As I chase the wind, it laughs so loud.
I stumbled on clovers, what a sight,
They waved their leaves, dusted with light.

Oh, what a stroll through blooms so bright,
Nature's own circus, a pure delight.
With every step, I share a grin,
This silly walk, let the fun begin!

Starlit Wanderings of the Soul

Beneath a sky where stars are bold,
I moonwalked right into a tale retold.
A shooting star winked, then spun away,
I tripped on starlight, oh what a play!

Constellations formed in funny shapes,
Like a cat in pajamas or a loaf of grapes.
I asked the moon for some wise advice,
It chuckled back, 'Add a sprinkle of spice!'

Comets zoomed by with a whoosh and a blast,
They laughed at my clumsiness, how fast!
I danced with shadows, swirling free,
But stepped on a cloud and dropped my tea!

Oh, wander on through this cosmic ride,
With laughter and stardust by my side.
Each twinkling laugh a tender song,
We float through the night, where we all belong!

Echoes of a Serene Odyssey

On a journey where the echoes play,
I met a parrot who had much to say.
It squawked in riddles and rhymes galore,
I answered back, 'What's behind that door?'

Walking on waves, a fish gave a cheer,
Told me the sea is full of good beer!
I took a sip from a jellyfish's cup,
The taste was strange – should I drink it up?

An octopus waved, its arms all askew,
It juggled shells like a circus crew.
I tried to join, but fell on my face,
The whole ocean burst out in a race!

What a voyage through realms untold,
With laughter resounding, both bright and bold.
In every echo, a joke unfurls,
In this serene whimsy, my spirit twirls!

Blossoms Beneath a Radiant Sky

Amidst the blooms where colors collide,
A sunflower joked, 'Watch your stride!'
I danced with tulips, had quite a ball,
Then tripped on a weed, how could I fall?

The poppies were laughing as I skipped by,
Their petals swaying like a bowtie sky.
I told a daisy that I loved its charm,
It giggled back, 'Just watch the farm!'

Beneath a canopy of rainbow delight,
Bees played hopscotch, oh what a sight!
I joined their game with a big wide grin,
But lost my turn, and the game wore thin!

So here's to blooms and the laughter they bring,
In the warm sun where the daisies sing.
With every petal, a joke takes flight,
Beneath this radiant, funny light!

Trails of Forgotten Harmony

On the path, I tripped on a shoe,
Found a sandwich, stale but not blue.
Laughter echoed, a bird took flight,
The sky was puzzling, not quite right.

A squirrel danced, his tail too grand,
Stole my snack, as if it was planned.
Giggles bounced on the bumpy road,
Life is strange, but it lightened the load.

Each twist and turn brought a rare bite,
Of wildly mismatched delight, what a sight!
Friends in laughter, we strolled along,
In funny mismatches, we found our song.

With every stumble, joy came grand,
As nature's jokes slipped through our hands.
We wandered, giggling till sundown,
In a world where silly wears the crown.

The Gentle Sway of Blissful Breezes

Leaves were dancing, they seemed to tease,
Rustling softly with the playful breeze.
I twirled around, tripped on my shoelace,
The wind just chuckled, put me in place.

Clouds laughed down, white fluff in the sky,
Chasing shadows as they floated by.
I tried to guide a butterfly's flight,
But it led me nowhere, what a sight!

Flowers giggled in colors so bright,
Whispering secrets to the fading light.
With every step, I'd burst out loud,
Funny moments made me so proud.

Oh what a pathway, where laughs align,
In the gentle sway, all's so divine.
With buddies beside me, we drift and sway,
Together we turn for a silly ballet.

Harvesting the Joyful Horizons

Fields of corn held an old scarecrow,
Who winked and winked with a toothy show.
He told me stories of crows gone wild,
As if he were some magical child.

We gathered pumpkins, round and fat,
One rolled away, and I gave chase, flat.
The laughter echoed across the patch,
Harvesting joy, no need to hatch.

Bouncing left and right like a goofy dance,
Every stumble given a second chance.
With smiles bright as the sun's warm glow,
Horizons shimmered wherever we'd go.

In fields where we gathered the fun of fall,
Life's a circus, come one, come all!
A merry band of thejoyful thrill,
Harvesting moments, laughter to spill.

Embracing the Mystical Wildflowers

In a meadow where oddities bloom,
I found a gnome with a polka-dot broom.
He tried to dance, slipped on his toes,
And twirled me in circles, oh where it goes!

Wildflowers giggled as they swayed,
Each petal a secret, lovingly played.
I joined the party that day with glee,
As bumblebees buzzed in harmony.

Colorful chaos painted the scene,
With petals weaving in the light, so keen.
We rolled on soft grass, laughter pure,
In mystic magic, we found our cure.

With every twist and turn around,
We gathered joy wherever it's found.
In this garden of laughter, we'd stay a while,
Embracing the weirdness with every smile.

Fragrant Footsteps

In a garden where the flowers bow,
The bees dance like they've found a vow.
A snail races, making quite a fuss,
While I sip tea, on a bench with rust.

Birds gossip loud, in a feathered chat,
A squirrel steals my sandwich—it's just flat!
I chase it down, but it's far too spry,
Guess I'll snack on crumbs and sigh with nigh.

Lizards sunbathe, plotting their next scheme,
While I ponder if I bought the right cream.
Each step a giggle, each turn a delight,
In this whacky stroll, there's never a fright.

So grab your hat, let's make it a spree,
With mishaps awaiting, oh, the glee!
In this fragrant land where laughter reigns,
We'll stroll 'til sunset, through silly terrains.

Radiant Retreat

On a beach where the sun wears a grin,
 I dig my toes in, feeling the win.
A crab waves hello, then scuttles away,
 In this radiant spot, who needs to play?

Seagulls squawk tales of lost French fries,
 While I laugh at the waves as they rise.
A toddler nearby starts building a moat,
 With a plastic shovel and a pirate's coat.

The ice cream truck's jingle brings me delight,
 I race to it, what a thrilling flight!
Strawberry, chocolate, or mint so sweet?
 This radiant treat just can't be beat!

As sun dips low, colors blend so fine,
With laughter around, it feels like a sign.
In this vibrant escape, joy takes the throne,
Oh, let's keep dancing, this place feels like home!

Ascending the Clouds

Up the hill where the air gets thin,
A goat with shades is ready to win.
It jumps and twists, oh what a sight,
As I huff and puff, trying with all my might.

The clouds are fluffy, like cotton candy,
I reach for one, it feels quite dandy.
A bird lands near, and gives me a wink,
I ponder if it's had too much to drink.

I trip on my laces—who ties these foes?
While the clouds just giggle, like everyone knows.
I point to the summit, "Is that where we go?"
But the goat just bleats, "You're too slow, too slow!"

As daylight fades and stars come out,
My adventure's a memory, without a doubt.
We may not reach high, but that's quite alright,
With laughter and joy, we've taken flight!

Pilgrimage of Joy

Pack your bags, bring your finest hat,
We're off on a journey, just imagine that!
With snacks galore and maps made of dreams,
This pilgrimage glows with silly extremes.

A riddle from a frog, can you solve it right?
While I trip on twigs, in a comedic fight.
The trees are all chuckling, rooting for me,
"Keep going, dear friend, you can't let it be!"

We stumble on jellybeans, bright and absurd,
While a cow on the hill simply goes unheard.
With each step we take, giggles intertwine,
In this funny parade, everything's fine!

At day's final whistle, we bask in the glow,
With stories and laughter, the best kind of show.
Though the path was absurd, our hearts feel so light,
This pilgrimage of joy makes everything bright.

Route to Reverie

In a land where socks don't match,
We skip and hop like a bouncy patch.
With jelly beans wrapped in silly hats,
We dance with squirrels, chatting with cats.

Through fields of giggles, we glide with grace,
Where ice cream flows in a happy place.
With chocolate rivers and cookie trees,
We laugh out loud, just like the bees.

We'll trip on rainbows and spin in glee,
While napping on clouds, we feel so free.
With popsicle paths and bubblegum skies,
We wander where every small thing flies.

Oh, what a joy to laugh and roam,
In this quirky spot we call our home.
With joy in our hearts and a jig in our feet,
Every step we take is a whimsical treat.

Sunkissed Sojourn

Beneath the sun, we prance like pals,
With flamingo hats and striped pink gals.
The sand tickles toes, oh what a tease,
As seagulls squawk, asking for cheese.

A beach ball bounces, it flies away,
Chasing a crab who joins our play.
With flip-flops clapping like a drum,
We're queens and kings, going on the run.

Sips of lemonade, sweet and bright,
Splashing in waves from morning till night.
We build castles that brush the sky,
With jellybean flags that flutter high.

As the sun dips low, we giggle and cheer,
Waving goodbye to our sunny sphere.
We dream of treasures, seashells in hand,
In this silly sojourn, oh isn't it grand?

Nirvana's Nexus

In a place where bananas wear shoes,
We party with kangaroos, singing the blues.
With smoothies that sparkle and rainbows that pop,
We twirl and whirl, we just can't stop.

Time flies on a turtle who can't quite race,
While sunflowers giggle, filling the space.
We skip over puddles of pink lemonade,
And swing from clouds in a fruity parade.

What joy erupts when muffin hats spin,
As we dance with the stars—let the fun begin!
With fireflies twinkling like tiny jewels,
We bask in the wonder, breaking all rules.

In this joyful junction, life's a good jest,
With laughter and mirth, oh, we feel so blessed!
So come take a trip, don't be shy and vex,
Join our merry maze at nirvana's next hex!

Twilight Tread

As dusk descends, we skip on air,
With dancing shadows that flip and flare.
We tiptoe past giggles, on a moonbeam's glow,
With silly wishes that make us grow.

The stars are our guides, winking away,
As we taste the ticks of a giddy display.
With glow-in-the-dark shoes, we prance and pounce,
In a game of giggles where we all bounce.

Through valleys of whispers and hills of cheer,
We toss all our worries without any fear.
With cupcakes in hand, we munch and play,
In this whimsical dance that won't go away.

In twilight's embrace, we tread so light,
With laughter echoing through the night.
Join our camaraderie, come take a chance,
In this funny place, let's whirl and prance!

Dreamer's Detour

On a road paved in marshmallow fluff,
I tripped on a cloud that was way too tough.
Sipped whipped cream from a fountain divine,
And danced with a squirrel who said, "Be mine!"

Rainbows rolled like tumbleweeds,
Bouncing past as I planted my seeds.
Lollipop trees grew gumdrops in rows,
While the wind whispered secrets only I chose.

Caught in a whirl of taffy and bliss,
I argued with shadows; they couldn't be missed.
My hat flew away, on a zephyr it soared,
But I just laughed loud and asked for more adored.

A slide made of licorice curved to the left,
I followed its path, feeling quite blessed.
With each silly stumble, I skated and spun,
On this whimsical path, oh, so much fun!

Sylvan Step

In a forest where giggles leap off the trees,
I stepped on a mushroom that wobbled like cheese.
Each critter wore hats, a sight to behold,
With fashion so funky, they made me feel bold.

A river of soda flowed sweetly nearby,
I dipped my toes in, in hopes I could fly.
The fish sang in harmony, what a display!
I joined in their chorus, hip-hop all the way.

Under a sky where cupcakes drifted by,
I chased after dreams as they danced in the sky.
Stumbled on waffles, oh what a delight,
In this forest of laughter, everything's bright!

And when the sun set, it melted like gold,
I knew this adventure had stories untold.
With my mismatched socks, I pranced down the lane,
In the sylvan steps, nothing's ever the same!

Passage Through Paradise

Through a door made of glitter, I skipped with a grin,
Where jellybean flowers bloomed thick as the din.
A parade of loud frogs sang sass all around,
I couldn't help chuckle at their croaky sound.

With ice cream mountains, so tall they could topple,
I climbed to the summit, a real sweetened wobble.
Marshmallow sheep grazed on candy cane grass,
While I rolled down the hill—oh, what a blast!

Caught in this whirlwind of sugary dreams,
I juggled with penguins who wore mighty beams.
Spinning like tops, they sent me up high,
Rocketing off as the cupcakes did fly.

In this passage of giggles, I found my way,
A ride on a donut made my heart sway.
With sprinkles of joy on a life oh so merry,
I danced with my shadow—it was light as a cherry!

Glimmers of Gleefulness

On a path made of giggles and dreams dipped in light,
    I stumbled on laughter; oh, what a sight!
    A jester of joy tipped his hat with a grin,
    Said, "Join me for tea, let the fun now begin!"

    Bouncing on bubbles that floated like flies,
    The trees were all chuckling, oh, what a surprise!
    With topsy-turvy daisies that danced in formation,
    I twirled with delight, such sheer jubilation!

    A pixie with sparkles threw snowflakes of cheer,
    Each flake told a story that tickled the ear.
    In this realm of elation, where silliness reigns,
    I spun in a whirlwind of giggles and gains.

As nightfall approached, the stars winked their charms,
    I waved to the moon, and it offered its arms.
    With glimmers of gleefulness blazing so bright,
    I danced through the evening, into pure delight!

Quest for Eden

In search of a place with fruits so sweet,
We tripped on the grass, and we faced defeat.
A squirrel stole our snacks, so sly and spry,
We laughed till we cried, oh me, oh my!

With flowers that danced and birds that prance,
We thought we could join, so we took a chance.
But slipped on a banana, oh what a sight,
A tumble, a giggle, right out of the light!

We climbed up a hill, or was it a mound?
Chasing a dream that was rarely found.
But a cow in the way said, "Do you mind?"
We thought we would stay, and let fate unwind.

The quest was absurd, but oh what a ride,
With laughter and fun, we went side by side.
In search of the garden, we found a good time,
So here's to the journey, oh how sublime!

Blissful Byways

Down blissful lanes where the sun likes to play,
We wandered and giggled, come what may.
With ice cream in hand, we just couldn't stop,
Till a pigeon swooped down, and it made a plop!

The flowers were whispering secrets so bright,
We tried a conga line, oh what a sight!
But we stepped on a bee, and it buzzed in surprise,
A dance we did twirl, yes, under sunny skies!

We met a wise tortoise who shared tales galore,
About chasing rainbows and sweet candy stores.
We cheered as he laughed, "I've seen it all,
But you young ones just trip, and that's the best call!"

Though roads may twist, and laughter may bend,
In our jolly hearts, we always transcend.
For on these happy byways, smiles linger and gleam,
We found joy in the journey, living the dream!

Arcadia Awaits

In fields of green where chickens trot,
We chased the breeze, we forgot what we sought.
With jelly on toast, and laughter on brew,
We danced with the daisies, as if we were new!

The sun wore a hat, that was slightly askew,
And bees buzzed along with their own rendezvous.
We played hopscotch with clouds and jumped over rain,
The nonsense of adulthood? A jovial strain!

Our footsteps were light as we twirled like mice,
Eating cake from the sky, oh isn't that nice?
But caught in our bliss, we forgot to look back,
At the snail who was racing with style and flair, what a whack!

Arcadia awaits with a wink and a wave,
A whimsical land where the silly lives brave.
So gather your giggles and come join the spree,
For the heart of this place is the laughter, you see!

Pathway of Petals

On a trail lined with petals and sticky glows,
We followed our noses where wild mint grows.
But tripping on petals, we found ourselves torn,
Giggling like children from dusk till dawn!

The path was a mystery, a riddle to crack,
With butterflies teasing, and all off the track.
We shouted, "Onward!" as we bumped into trees,
Only to find flowers that giggled with glee!

The sun peeked through clouds with a wink from afar,
We stumbled on puddles, slipped under the bar.
With splashes and squeals, we danced in the rain,
A pathway of petals, our dreams uncontained!

So let's cheese with the daisies, and toast with the sun,
This journey we share is all laughter and fun.
For the petals beneath us can't hold a frown,
As we skip on this path of joy all around!

Splendor Stroll

In a land where daisies talk,
And tulips wear their finest frock,
I tripped on grass, a sight to see,
A squirrel giggled right at me.

With crickets playing in the band,
And bumblebees, oh so grand,
I danced along the winding lane,
Then slipped on mud, oh what a gain!

A goat in shades tapped to the beat,
He pulled a prank, like moving feet,
I laughed so hard I lost my hat,
Then chased a butterfly, imagine that!

Just down the path, a fountain flows,
Where rubber ducks put on their shows,
I clapped and cheered, it felt so right,
The sun was setting, it was a delight!

Meadow of Marvels

In a meadow filled with sights so bright,
The flowers bonked me, what a fright!
A butterfly bumped into my nose,
And daisies sneezed, oh how they rose!

The bunnies danced, a jig or two,
While grasshoppers sang the latest tune,
I joined the show, a wild debut,
Then lost my shoe—oh, what a coup!

With sunshine warm and clouds in line,
A snail offered me some lemon-lime,
I sipped and giggled at his slow affair,
As ladybugs twirled in the fresh, sweet air!

As twilight dropped a curtain low,
I whispered jokes to the willow,
The stars lit up, a comical scene,
In this meadow of marvels, oh so keen!

Whispering Woods Venture

In the woods where whispers twine,
A woodpecker challenged me, 'You're fine!'
I stumbled on roots, nearly fell,
The trees all chuckled, 'What the hell?'

A raccoon passed with snacks galore,
He winked and said, 'Want to score?'
I tried a chip, my taste buds cheered,
But the crunch was loud—now they all feared!

An owl hooted wise tales old,
While squirrels pranced, so bold and gold,
I tried to dance, but what a mess,
I ended up in a leafy dress!

As shadows danced and night crept near,
I found a bear with no fear,
He swayed with me, such silly grace,
In these whispering woods, a joyous place!

Blissful Wanderlust

With each step on this winding lane,
I found a shoe—lay just plain!
The birds joined in, a chorus loud,
As I juggled apples, feeling proud.

A snail raced by with speed unseen,
While pine cones tumbled, what a scene!
I dodged a frog, he waved and croaked,
In blissful wanderlust, smiles evoked.

As squirrels played tag with a hat so red,
I chased them down, no fear or dread,
I twirled and spun, my heart on fire,
While daisies clapped, they'd never tire!

A picnic spread on grass so green,
I sang aloud, like I was queen,
With cookie crumbs and laughter rife,
In this wild journey that's filled with life!

Breaths of Beauty

A chicken crossed the road, they say,
To find a spot where she'd roam and play.
With feathers fluffed and a waddle so spry,
She danced on a line, oh my, oh my!

The daisies giggled, the sun wore a grin,
As butterflies flitted, all around her spun.
She twirled with the daisies, a goofy ballet,
In a world that spun silly, hip-hip-hooray!

Breeze tickled her beak, she let out a squawk,
Joined by a goat who preferred to talk.
"Why are we here, just dance and be free?"
She clucked with delight, "It's pure comedy!"

With a hop and a skip, they formed quite a crew,
In a field of wildflowers, where laughter just grew.
The moral, it seems, is quite clear to see,
Life's best for the silly, just like you and me!

Realm of Resplendence

In a land where socks never lost their pair,
A wizard danced with a wild, green hair.
He whisked up some giggles, stirred them with flair,
And made magic muffins that floated in air!

The trees wore spectacles, reading with glee,
While worms played chess, as wise as can be.
A raccoon in a tux made an impromptu plea,
"Can I join in the fun? I'm curious, you see!"

Clouds shaped like donuts drifted and swayed,
While jellybeans rained down, a sugary parade.
The sun burst forth laughter, as warm as the day,
In this realm of resplendence, come join, don't delay!

A snail on a scooter sped by like a jet,
Challenging rabbits, who'd easily fret.
"Who's fastest?" they wondered, "Oh place your bet!"
But the real winners, my friend, were the snacks they beget!

Alignment of Auras

In a world where cats could finally talk,
They held secret meetings by the old backyard dock.
They'd align their auras with a sprinkle of charm,
Swapping tales of mischief and rigging the farm.

A dog named Rufus, with a heart bold and bright,
Joined in the banter, much to their delight.
"That fish over there said he'd leap and take flight,
But I'm holding my breath, it don't feel quite right!"

The squirrels in jackets exchanged gala news,
"Next week, we're hosting a nuts and fruit snooze!"
With acorns adorned, they would dance without shoes,
In an aura alignment of joyful hues!

By sunset they cuddled, under stars twinkling high,
The moon made a cameo, twirling nigh.
With laughter echoing through the moonlit sky,
In a world where all critters were oh-so spry!

Sublime Steps

On roads paved with candy, skip past the gloom,
Where gumdrops abound and giggles consume.
A pickle in shades with a smile so bright,
Led the parade on this sugary night.

The marshmallows danced with gusto and flair,
While licorice lassos soared high in the air.
"Join us!" they beckoned with sugary stare,
"To taste all that's lovely and shrug off the wear!"

A chocolate fountain bubbled with cheers,
As sprinkles confetti'd across all the peers.
Balloons filled with giggles, oh what a sphere!
In sublime steps taken, let's dance without fears!

So under the stars, with a twirl and a leap,
The candy parade promised laughter and keep.
Embrace all the whimsy, let your heart sweep,
And savor each moment, the sweetness so deep!

In Search of Celestial Shores

I packed my bags with snacks and cheer,
To find a place where cows hold dear.
But all I found were ducks in a row,
Quacking tales of the ocean's glow.

I chased a rainbow on a bicycle,
Wore sunglasses, feeling quite radical.
But stumbled on a muddy old bog,
And emerged looking like a wet dog.

I honked at clouds, so fluffy and wide,
But they just laughed and floated with pride.
The sun rolled eyes, said, "Nice try, dude!"
While I practiced my cartwheel with food.

So here I stand, with a grin on my face,
Embracing the nuttiness of this wondrous place.
With memories stored like jellybean jars,
I'll dance with the fireflies and count the stars.

A Tapestry of Radiant Footprints

I skipped along a wobbly path,
In search of joy, and a little math.
But numbers gave way to candy canes,
And giggles erupted like wild champagne.

Footprints shimmered with a fruity smell,
Leading me to a whimsical carousel.
I hopped on a horse that wore a hat,
And laughed as it danced with a giant cat.

We twirled through trees that whispered sweet,
Telling me stories while tapping my feet.
A chorus of crickets joined in the fun,
As I strummed a tune on a rubbery bun.

So here's to the trails where laughter ignites,
Where surprises await and dancing delights.
I'll weave those footprints into my song,
As we all march together, where we belong.

The Enchanted Passage of Light

I stumbled upon a glowing surprise,
A trail of cupcakes that danced in the skies.
With sprinkles and frosting, my stomach went wild,
As I bounded ahead like a sugar-fueled child.

Beneath the glow of a moon made of cheese,
I found my old socks, just flapping in the breeze.
They whispered secrets of pie-eating contests,
While raccoons nearby prepared for their quests.

A parade of shadows began to parade,
Unicycles and llamas, a grand charade!
Nature giggled, the stars joined the show,
As marshmallows rained down in a soft, fluffy flow.

So I danced through that magical, glowing night,
Embracing the silly, absorbing the light.
With joy in my heart, I was ready to play,
In this jest of a journey, come what may.

Surrendering to Nature's Embrace

I wandered where flowers wear funky hats,
And squirrels host concerts with jazzy chats.
The trees threw a party, we all wore crowns,
While frogs in tuxedos croaked silly sounds.

With every step, I tripped on a joke,
As daisies giggled, and played a hoax.
They tickled my toes with their wiggly stems,
And dared me to dance with my furry friends.

The breeze tossed confetti from leaves overhead,
As I laughed and twirled, feeling playful instead.
The moon winked at me from its cozy seat,
While shadows joined in, moving to the beat.

So I surrendered to nature's wild jest,
Finding giggles and magic, on this merry quest.
With every chuckle, and each rolling spring,
I'll embrace the delight that adventure can bring.

Impromptu Invocations

In a land where the chickens sing,
And squirrels wear tiny rings.
Misplaced socks dance in delight,
As we stumble into the night.

The ducks hold court in a tree,
Debating how to sip their tea.
Meanwhile, a goat sings out loud,
Leaving everyone quite proud.

With each step, we trip on air,
Chasing giggles beyond compare.
A butterfly steals our popcorn,
Shouting, 'Hey! This isn't forlorn!'

Through fields of giggles and glee,
We lose our shoes, but not esprit.
An unexpected slide greets our feet,
As we tumble into a sugary treat.

Twilight Treads

Underneath the moon's soft gleam,
The cat serenades a dream.
Bouncing rabbits dance in style,
While we wander and just smile.

A tree-shaped cake stands so tall,
With frosting that invites us all.
We climb for bites, but oh, what fun,
As ants declare, 'We're not done!'

The stars pop like bubblegum,
As we race the night, oh so dumb!
Each light twinkles a cheeky laugh,
While we prance on a flower's path.

Into the dark, we brave the odd,
Frogs croak jokes that feel quite broad.
We toss our cares to the breeze,
Cackling as we trip on peas.

Eden's Embers

In a garden of pies and fun,
Where apples skate and flowers run.
We pluck a giggle from the vines,
And sip on juice of silly signs.

A talking pot plants wise cracks,
While we detour on rubber tracks.
Cucumbers claiming their debates,
As lettuce spins on roller skates.

Fireflies wink with crafty grins,
As we race against our chins.
A sharp-tongued parrot cracks the code,
Yelling, 'This is the funny road!'

With every step, a laugh unwinds,
In this realm where joy reminds.
We tumble into leaves of gold,
As the night's wild tales unfold.

Wandering into Wonder

Through fields of marshmallows we glide,
Where gummy bears choose to hide.
Bouncing clouds play silly tunes,
As we dance beneath big balloons.

A hedgehog reads a bedtime story,
While we chuckle, lost in glory.
The sun winks with a cheeky ray,
Inviting us to roll and play.

With each hop, jelly beans sprout,
As our laughter turns about.
We chase the giggles, nothing meek,
Finding treasure with every squeak.

The moon throws confetti in delight,
While we twirl in purest flight.
In this realm, ordinary's a blast,
As fun overcomes us, at last.

Tranquil Trails

Where rivers giggle and tumble down,
The squirrels wear sunglasses in this sleepy town.
Flowerpots dance, they move to the beat,
And the daisies sneak cookies, oh what a treat!

Breezes tell jokes, they wiggle and sway,
While butterflies paint graffiti, what do you say?
The sun plays hide and seek with the trees,
As frogs practice yoga with great expertise!

Hopping along, we trip on our shoes,
Chasing our shadows while singing the blues.
A picnic of pickles, with marshmallows too,
In this world of wonder, we laugh and we woo!

So come take a stroll, let worries be few,
In this land of giggles where skies are so blue.
Every step holds a chuckle, every turn brings delight,
On these tranquil trails, oh what a sight!

Avenue of Dreams

Down the avenue where umbrellas dance,
Epic kangaroo parties give life a chance.
Bubblegum trees give the sweetest of blooms,
While pizza slice clouds sail over cartoon rooms.

A raccoon in a tux offers you some cheese,
With apples in top hats, oh what a tease!
Caterpillars strut, looking sharp and neat,
While the puddles reflect our unconventional feet.

Lollipops rain, and everyone grins,
Jogging on jelly, we've all got our spins.
The sun shines in polka dots, quite absurd,
While a chorus of crickets sings gossip unheard.

So take a leap, let your spirit soar,
On this whimsical avenue, there's always more.
Adventure awaits in every silly scene,
Laughter is found where the joy is routine!

Celestial Crossroads

At celestial crossroads where stars wear shoes,
Planets throw parties, there's nothing to lose.
Galaxies gossip, they twinkle and beam,
While comets craft cupcakes, oh what a dream!

Aliens juggling in bright neon lights,
Host cosmic picnics on warm summer nights.
Moons cracking jokes, with rings made of cheese,
As space cats play chess with effortless ease.

Time takes a nap, it's feeling quite lazy,
And clocks do the cha-cha, oh aren't they crazy?
Sunbeams are giggling, giving high fives,
In this interstellar, where laughter thrives!

So come spin around, let your worries drift,
In this starry playground, feel the cosmic shift.
Every twinkle's a tickle, each orbit a jest,
At these celestial crossroads, life's simply the best!

Oasis of Light

In the oasis of light, where shadows take breaks,
Lions sip lattes and hang out with snakes.
Cacti wear sombreros, quite the bold sight,
As the sun does the limbo, feeling just right.

Mirages tell tales, with a wink and a grin,
While camels wear vests, letting the fun begin.
Dunes dance like dancers, all humming a tune,
And the sand starts to sparkle beneath the bright moon.

Bouncing balloons float down sandy blue trails,
While parrots flip pancakes to set all the scales.
Palm trees tap their toes, keeping the beat,
In this cheer-filled oasis, life's oh so sweet!

So come share a giggle, feel the sun's gentle kiss,
In this light-filled enclave, it's a wonderful bliss.
Every moment's a laugh, every breeze brings delight,
In this oasis of light, the world feels just right!

Enchanted Passage

Through woods of giggles, we skip and sway,
With squirrels all dressed in their Sunday best,
A raccoon in sunglasses steals the display,
As we dance with rabbits, life feels like a jest.

A brook babbles jokes, whispers of glee,
While frogs in bowties croak out the fun,
Beneath the tall oaks, wild spirits run free,
Chasing each other, oh, we won the pun!

If you spot a fox, just watch out for pranks,
In this lively land, mischief is king,
With each step we take, we give our heart thanks,
For the laughter and joy that the critters bring.

So come join the revels, leave worries behind,
Here in this space where the silly blooms,
The path's made of giggles, so bright and unconfined,
Let's frolic together, in colorful rooms.

Sanctuary of the Soul

Under the sunshine, we stumble and roam,
Where butterflies chuckle at silly old bees,
A hedgehog with humor will take us back home,
As he juggles some mushrooms with uproarious ease.

The flowers are gossiping, swaying about,
With petals that tickle and whisper sweet lines,
A snail in a top hat prances about,
Cracking jokes about weather and fanciful signs.

In this whimsical haven, no troubles can stay,
With clouds that play tag and giggle like kids,
Let's dance with the daisies, shake off the gray,
And join in the laughter that nature forbids.

Here in this refuge, oh can't you see,
Every giggle blooms right from the ground,
In the sanctuary where laughter runs free,
The soul finds its song in the joyful surround.

Realm of Radiance

In a garden of chuckles, the daisies all show,
As they bloom with the laughter of bees on the wing,
A sunflower grins wide, putting on quite a show,
With petals like confetti, it can't help but sing.

Clouds roll like giggles, fluffy and bright,
While rainbows do somersaults, shining so bold,\nThe sun
plays hide-and-seek, what a fun sight,
As a troupe of elves juggles glittering gold.

There's mischief in the breeze, whispers of cheer,
With a turtle in slippers taking a stroll,
Sailing on leaves, oh it's perfectly clear,
The joy of this place tickles deep in the soul.

So take off your shoes, feel the warmth on your feet,
Join the frolicsome dance with a jubilant spirit,
In this realm of delight, make your heart skip a beat,
With laughter and light, come on, let's near it.

Harmony's Route

On paths lined with laughter, we march to a beat,
With nuts in our pockets, a picnic in tow,
The critters around us, they laugh and repeat,
Every curious story that they want us to know.

A parrot named Polly is quite the wise sage,
Cracking up rhymes with a flamboyant flare,
While bees do the cha-cha, they're setting the stage,
In a world where absurdity dances in air.

The river flows songs, with its bubbly delight,
Conveying the gossip of rocks down below,
Where fish sport a tie and flash a big smile,
It's a whimsical ride, let's enjoy every row.

So gather your friends, let's follow the fun,
Checkered with laughter, our burdens'll fade,
In harmony's bliss, we bask in the sun,
On this route where the silly-drawn serenade.

www.ingramcontent.com/pod-product-compliance
Lightning Source LLC
Chambersburg PA
CBHW072214070526
44585CB00015B/1331